ASKING

*A 59-Minute Guide to Everything
Board Members, Volunteers, and Staff
Must Know to Secure the Gift*

Companion Book to Asking

FUND RAISING REALITIES EVERY BOARD MEMBER MUST FACE

A 1-Hour Crash Course on Raising Major Gifts for Nonprofit Organizations

David Lansdowne
FOREWORD BY JEROLD PANAS

NEW, REVISED EDITION

Among the Top Three Bestselling Fundraising Books of All Time

If every board member of every nonprofit organization across America read this book, it's no exaggeration to say that millions upon millions of additional dollars would be raised.

How could it be otherwise when, after spending just *one* hour with this gem, board members everywhere would understand virtually everything they need to know about raising major gifts. Not more, not less. Just exactly what they need to do to be successful.

In his bestselling book, *Fund Raising Realities Every Board Member Must Face: A 1-Hour Crash Course on Raising Major Gifts for Nonprofit Organizations*, David Lansdowne has distilled the essence of major gifts fundraising, put it in the context of 47 "realities," and delivered it in unfailingly clear prose.

Nothing about this book will intimidate board members. It is brief, concise, easy to read, and free of all jargon. Further, it's a work that motivates, showing just how doable raising big money is.

The appeal of *Fund Raising Realities* is that Lansdowne addresses every important principle and technique of fund raising, and explains them in a succinct way board members will grasp immediately. In other words, *Fund Raising Realities* puts everyone on a level playing field - board member with board member, and board member with staff.

Put this book in your board's hands, put it in your board orientation packet, put it anywhere you need the successful practice of fundraising masterfully illuminated.

From Emerson & Church, Publishers
www.emersonandchurch.com

ASKING

A 59-Minute Guide to Everything
Board Members, Volunteers, and Staff
Must Know to Secure the Gift

JEROLD PANAS

Foreword by Bonnie McElveen-Hunter

Emerson
& Church
PUBLISHERS

First printed January 2009

10 9 8 7 6 5 4 3 2 1

Printed in the United States of America

This text is printed on acid-free, FSC certified paper.

Emerson & Church, Publishers
P.O. Box 338 • Medfield, MA 02052
Tel. 508-359-0019 • Fax 508-359-2703
www.emersonandchurch.com

Library of Congress Cataloging-in-Publication Data

Panas, Jerold.
  Asking : a 59-minute guide to everything board members, volunteers, and staff must know to secure the gift / Jerold Panas. — Rev. ed.
    p. cm.
  ISBN 1-889102-35-0 (pbk. : alk. paper)
  1. Fund raising—Handbooks, manuals, etc. 2. Gifts—Handbooks, manuals, etc. 3. Nonprofit organizations—Finance—Handbooks, manuals, etc. I. Title.
  HG177.P358 2009
  658.15'224—dc22
                                    2008046544

FOREWORD

Have you ever sat in a board meeting and had an exciting idea shelved for lack of funds?

Have you ever watched the creative imagination of your CEO shrivel after a finance report took the wind out of her sails?

Have you ever been asked to take part in a fundraising effort for an organization you believe in, but begged off because you hate asking for money?

If you've had any of these experiences, this book is for you.

Start reading it and your uneasiness and discomfort with asking for money will begin to fade. I guarantee it! Why? Because Jerry Panas is a master at making fundraising simple. He even makes it fun! He'll get you laughing, and before long you'll start to believe you *can* do it!

In fact, his words inspired me to begin a Women's Leadership Giving Initiative that today has raised over $500 million dollars and that's just the beginning. With Jerry as your mentor you can do it, too!

In *Asking*, Jerry shows you how to earn a gift, step by step. He gives you the words to say on the phone, what to write in a note to get the appointment, and what to say when you meet with the potential donor. You can't beat that. He also gives you practical and even humorous responses to the excuses and objections you'll inevitably hear.

As Chairman of the Board of the American Red Cross, I have seen Jerry in action. I've watched him inspire our Board of Governors to the point they were practically standing on tiptoes with anticipation! Most of all, I've watched Jerry teach our board the greatest fundraising lesson of all – that it is a privilege to give. Giving changes lives and save lives, and as a result the arts are funded, people are fed, children learn to read, and families have shelter. The immense good that's achieved by asking cannot be measured.

I close with this analogy. Have you ever been to a musical performance that was so fabulous you just had to tell people about it? That's the way I feel about this book. It is so wonderful that once you read it you'll start to fall in love with fundraising and with Jerry Panas. And you, too, will change lives.

With anticipation for what this book will do for you and for our world,

Bonnie McElveen-Hunter   Greensboro, NC

Editor's Note: Bonnie McElveen-Hunter, former U.S. Ambassador to the Republic of Finland, is the Founder and CEO of Pace Communications, ranked by Working Woman Magazine as one of the top 175 women-owned businesses. Bonnie currently serves as Chairman of the American Red Cross, the first woman to be selected in the organization's 100-plus year history. She has also served as a member of the International Board of Directors of Habitat for Humanity, chaired the Alexis de Tocqueville Society and is a founder of the United Way Billion Dollar National Women's Leadership Initiative.

CONTENTS

1

THE JOY OF ASKING!

———■———

A fundraiser stood at the heavenly gate,
His face was scarred and old.
He stood before the man of fate
For admission to the fold.
"What have you done," Saint Peter said,
"To gain admission here?"
"I've been a fundraiser, sir,
"For many and many a year."
The pearly gates swung open wide,
Saint Peter rang the bell.
"Come in and choose your harp," he sighed,
"You've had your share of hell!"

2

THANKS FOR BEING A FRIEND

———■———

Congratulations.

You're among the greatest and the most privileged. You're about to undertake what George Bernard Shaw called, "The joy of being used for a purpose recognized by all as a mighty one."

You've shown your willingness to call on others for a cause of great importance. You'll be talking with friends, business colleagues, and perhaps even some people you don't know well.

That's what makes fundraising and your involvement so critically important, and at the same time such great fun.

Your task is vital because without your help your organization couldn't exist. It couldn't balance its budget, provide its services, couldn't build the buildings. You make it possible.

And your task is fun. Yes, just plain fun. Because everyone you call on will have a different feeling about giving, a different perception of your organization.

Each person will be in a different position financially, and will be experiencing different stresses and strains, singular joys, and motivations.

No presentation will be the same as the next. And I can almost promise you none will follow the exact scenario you planned.

But that's not important. Because what I've discovered in all my years of fundraising is that it almost doesn't matter how you ask -- although I'll give you some tips and suggestions in this book. What's important is that you ask. Just do it.

There's no such thing as an incorrect ask. Maybe it could've been done more effectively, more strategically and perhaps more deftly. But the important thing is that you ask. That's what really counts. And that you do it with enthusiasm and commitment.

I've also learned that no matter how dazzling your presentation, not everyone will give. Or the gift may not be at the level you had hoped.

This can be disappointing. The pain can be so great, it can hurt you into poetry! But what keeps you going is that you did your best.

Get ready for the great adventure. Because of you and the funds you raise, you'll be directly responsible, through your organization, for changing lives. You are making it happen.

Andrew Golden, the songwriter, wrote *Thank You for Being a Friend*. He could have dedicated that song to you.

3

YOU'RE NEVER A LOSER UNTIL YOU QUIT TRYING

—————■—————

For me, one of the great satisfactions is asking men and women to invest in compelling causes and audacious dreams. You're going to feel the same way.

I find that the really difficult part in fundraising isn't getting people to give. That's actually easy. The tough part for many volunteers is asking.

But, as you'll learn in these pages, asking for a gift shouldn't cause trembling and timid hearts. It isn't selling. It isn't razzle-dazzle or persuading someone to do something he doesn't want to do. It's mostly having people simply do the right thing.

Keep in mind that men and women don't want to give money away. They want to invest in great causes, in bold and exciting dreams. They want to feel they're helping change lives and save lives. It's your job to help them understand their money can make that happen ... with a little help from you.

Don't worry about techniques and tools. What's far more important is having the right instincts. Keep your antennae alert and vibrating. Positive results will follow.

And don't be concerned about not being an expert at this. Keep in mind that the Titanic was built by an expert and Noah's Ark by a rank amateur.

In his career, Michael Jordan said he missed nearly 10,000 shots, lost over 3,000 games, and missed making the decisive shot dozens of times. "I've failed over and over in my life ... and that's why I succeeded."

On those occasions when you don't get the gift -- and there will be those times -- it wasn't your presentation that failed. You gave it your best, you made the ask, you fought hard for the cause. You didn't stumble, say the wrong things, or fail to follow the script. None of that.

Some men and women simply will not give. That's not your failure, it's theirs.

4

YOU WON'T GET MILK FROM A COW BY SENDING A LETTER

———■———

I had just finished speaking and if I must say so, it was one of my better days. The group was responsive, they laughed in the proper places, and I ended with something that resounded like Tchaikovsky's 1812 Overture.

People were on their feet applauding. A standing ovation! It was a blessed moment. As Tennessee Williams said: "I felt as though I had just inherited the sky."

In a sense, these were my kind of people, a meeting of 500 or so Seventh-day Adventists, institutional leaders from all over the world. CEOs from hospitals, colleges, and schools. I've managed so many programs for the Church I feel like an Adventist myself (I could even become one if it weren't for the prohibition on coffee).

When the applause died down, Milton Murray, master of ceremonies, got up to thank me.

"Jerry, you've meant so much to so many institutions of our Church, we've decided to do something special for you. We're going to name a Chair in your honor."

A Chair! A named-Chair. In my honor. I was stunned. I knew I'd have to respond in some way but as I began pushing my chair back, there wasn't a single thought in my head. A total blank. All I could think of was the admonition: "Forget the cheese -- just find a way to get out of the trap."

Milton continued talking as I walked toward the podium to accept my honor.

"Well, it isn't exactly a Chair," he said. From behind the table, Milton produced a stool and held it high above his head.

I looked at Milton and the stool. ("Cripes, what's this all about?")

"It's just what it looks like, Jerry, a milking stool. And on it is a brass plaque in your honor. We're giving you this because you've taught us so well."

By this time, I was at the podium, Milton congratulating me and pumping my hand. He read the plaque. It was an admonishment from Si Seymour, the great doyen of our profession. It said:

"You won't get milk from a cow by sending a letter. And you won't get milk by calling on the phone. The only way to get milk from a cow is to sit by its side and milk it."

Let Seymour's words be a lesson to you. Remember them well. You won't get a gift, at least not of any size, by sending a letter. And you won't get a gift by calling on the telephone, not of the size you want.

To get a gift at the level required, you're going to have to call on the prospect in person.

Sit by that cow and milk it!

5

ENTHUSIASM IS CONTAGIOUS, START AN EPIDEMIC

—————■—————

What are the factors that will make you successful and effective as a fundraiser?

Is it salesmanship -- your ability to persuade someone of the merits of the project by the sheer weight of your eloquence and the dazzling flow of words? Or is it that you know the prospect so well, it's hard to say no to you?

I needed to know what makes a great fundraiser.

So I conducted a number of focus groups among men and women who recently gave large sums. Here's the nature of the questions we probed:

- What can you remember about the man or woman who called on you (whether a friend, staff person, casual acquaintance, or someone you didn't know)? What stands out most in your mind?

- What was it that made that person an effective solicitor? We assume the cause and the institution are important to you, but what was it about the solicitor you liked most? What impressed you most?

Here's what I found. I call it my *Three Es*: Empathy, Energy, and Enthusiasm. These are the qualities the donors all talked about.

The need to be heard is one of the most powerful motivating forces in human nature. The donors we spoke with commended the solicitor for truly listening. The caller somehow entered into the donor's world and experience.

I was reminded just the other day how listening is directly linked to empathy. I was digging through an old file and came across a newspaper clipping I've saved for years. The date was 1933.

It's a photograph of Franklin Roosevelt, leaning on his cane, bent markedly forward, listening intently to two ragged men, perhaps homeless, who appear to have stopped him. The caption underneath the photograph reads: "He knows how to listen."

That's your role as a solicitor -- to listen. And that's how donors in our focus groups identified empathy. They want to be heard! Studies are clear on the subject: people care greatly about those who listen to them.

The next of the *Three Es* is energy. Time and time again in the focus groups, our donors talked about the energy their fundraiser brought to the visit. They said there were sparks.

18

The most powerful weapon on earth is the human soul on fire. It's what Robert Frost called "that immense energy of life which sparks a fire."

I find this true in all of the effective fundraisers. There's a highly charged energy. You feel surrounded by it. Like being in the eye of a tornado.

The really good fundraisers have some internal reservoir. They're able to bring forth a torrent of energy. And then to forge on and on for unlimited periods.

Donors said the callers they liked best all seemed to be peak performers, filled with intense and concentrated energy. They weren't talking about nervous energy, but the kind that exudes enthusiasm and joy.

Enthusiasm is the third "E." Everyone in my focus groups spoke about it. It's probably the ingredient that was the most telling and effective in the asking-mix.

Enthusiasm comes from two Greek words. First, there is 'theos,' which means God. The prefix 'en' means "within you." Enthusiasm: God within you. And that seems to be what all of the donors felt from their solicitor.

Unbridled, unflinching, undying enthusiasm -- the great fundraisers are driven by it. A magnificent presentation, dazzling literature, even a great cause -- none of this would matter if there weren't enthusiasm. It's what is called, "working near the heart of things."

Empathy. Energy. Enthusiasm. It's your job to bring these qualities to the solicitation.

19

But there's one last factor, and all of the donors we interviewed spoke of it. They can feel it. It permeates everything the fundraiser does and says. And that is ... Integrity. You never tamper with the truth.

Integrity is the mightiest weapon in the fundraiser's arsenal -- more important than the campaign literature or anything that is said. Its power is explosive.

Integrity alone is no assurance of getting the gift. But without it, you can't even begin the journey. You are a cannon, ready to be fired -- but without ammunition.

6

ENLIGHTENED GIVERS FEEL THE RAPTURE OF BEING ALIVE

---■---

If you make enough calls, you're bound to meet and talk with a number of wonderful and generous men and women. Within that group, you're certain, sooner or later, to come across a category I call enlightened-givers.

That's part of the wonderful joy of being a solicitor -- the extraordinary men and women you meet. In my experience, here's what I've found to be true of the enlightened-givers. You'll meet more of this kind than the others, I promise.

1. For enlightened-givers, there's a sense that they're only trustees of the money they've earned or inherited. They find it wonderful fun to give money to help those in need. They find making a gift to be a rollicking experience.

2. They love to give. They would much rather say yes than no, even though there are times they have to reject a request. They're pleased to know that their money is going to help change lives.

3. They feel they don't have to give to every request, but they're willing to listen. These enlightened-givers, they never refuse to be solicited. They know that people who refuse to see a solicitor miss one of the great rewards in life.

4. They don't put it off. They see the solicitor as quickly as possible. Enlightened-givers understand the role of the fundraiser. They realize that asking is every bit as important as giving. They feel fundraisers should be shown great regard, encouragement, unending admiration, and deep gratitude. And the enlightened-givers heap it on.

5. Enlightened-givers realize that early gifts are the most important. They know that their quick commitment is infinitely more helpful to an organization than a late one. They give an answer as promptly as possible. And they don't put off their decision or force the solicitor to make repeated calls to find out the answer.

6. Enlightened-givers consider carefully their role in the campaign and what their gift might mean in terms of inspiring others to higher levels. And at times, they give more than they were asked for. Yes, more!

Once I asked a prospect to consider a gift of $100,000. She said: "No, I'll give you $500,000." I didn't express any obvious surprise, but in truth I was delightfully shocked.

I mentioned that this was a very special gift and more than was typical for her. "Every once in awhile, I try to give more than I'm asked for," she responded, "just for the sheer fun of it."

7. Enlightened-givers not only make the gift but they care so heartily about the cause and program, they decide to become personally involved.

As Kenneth Dayton said: "This has to be one of life's greatest joys and satisfactions -- to both volunteer and give money." And Ken was an enlightened-giver, virtually without parallel.

7

IT'S EASIER TO GET THE GIFT THAN THE VISIT

———■———

Now you're ready to begin.

You'll find that one of the most difficult steps in getting the gift is actually not the face-to-face presentation. And it's not that special moment when you actually ask for the gift.

What's most difficult is getting the visit.

Ah, that's the tough part. It takes steely determination and persistence and unyielding resolve. All of those. But, as I've discovered, if you find a path with no obstacles, it probably doesn't lead anywhere.

Here's the good news. When you get the visit, you're *85 percent* on your way to getting the gift. All of our studies indicate this.

Note, I don't call this an appointment. That may

seem like a small matter but as we know in this business of asking, success is in the details. An appointment has a negative connotation. If you need to have a root canal, you call your dentist for an appointment. Or maybe a proctologist you call for an appointment, if that's your particular need!

But a visit, that's quite different, quite pleasant. And this call for a visit should be the first step in a joyful journey. You're giving your prospect an opportunity to invest in saving lives, in changing lives. What could be more ennobling, more rewarding than that?

Always send a letter in advance of calling for a visit. I've worried about this. Will the letter actually prompt some turn-downs or make it impossible to get through on the phone? Does it give the prospect extra time to prepare arguments for closing off a visit?

I can assure you that sending a letter is the most effective way possible of securing the visit. And on top of everything else, it does save five or ten minutes in trying to explain on the phone why you want to see the person.

I'm going to give you three letters you can use as a guide. These will be most effective if you tweak them to sound more like you.

The first letter (*see Letter 1 in the Appendix*) should go on your (the volunteer's) stationery. It's more effective that way and far more likely to be opened.

This letter is an example of when you're using a staff person to arrange for your visits.

The second letter (*Letter 2 in the Appendix*) goes out on your stationery as well. This one is to be used when you're opening the door for a staff person to make the call on her own. It's an excellent letter, very effective, when there simply aren't enough volunteers to call on everyone.

But turning to staff is a fall-back position. Nothing is more effective than a volunteer making the call, or a staff person and a volunteer teaming up to make the call. I call the latter the *"Magic Partnership."*

The third letter (*Letter 3 in the Appendix*) is best of all and most effective. It's to be used when you're calling to make the arrangements for your own visit.

Note that in all of the letters, you've very clear you won't be asking for a gift. No – not on this visit!

There are two reasons for this. First of all, I find that by assuring the person the visit is entirely exploratory and interpretive, you're much more likely to get to see him or her.

And secondly, it's a good technique since it's almost certain you're going to need two visits to get the gift at the amount you hope for.

8

SUCCESSFUL PEOPLE DO WHAT OTHERS NEVER GET AROUND TO

———■———

Setting the visit can be tough. I know how difficult it is.

I've been raising funds for a long time and I agonize more about making the phone call for the visit than I do the actual presentation to the prospect.

So don't be concerned if you feel pangs of anxiety. I've found that without challenge, there's no achievement. Remember, when you get the visit you're 85 percent on your way to getting the gift.

Here are the steps necessary to ease those palpitations and help ensure that you get to see the person.

1. Send the type of letter I've recommended. Be certain to revise it in any way that helps make it your own.

2. Practice (practice, practice) your opening. Even with all my years, I still write out what I'm going to say on the phone.

3. Even though I use a script, so to speak, I don't read it of course. It has to sound spontaneous. But writing it out means I don't miss anything. And the truth is, the script gives me confidence. Keep in mind Churchill's admonition: "I have to practice a great deal in order to make a speech sound spontaneous."

4. Have a calendar handy. Remember, your purpose in making the call is to set the date for the visit. Get ready.

5. This is probably the most difficult part of all. Have you ever done this? You stare at the phone. Minutes go by. You know at some point you have to punch in the numbers. But you hope someone will phone, so you won't have to make the dreaded call. But the telephone doesn't ring.

Resolve that you'll fling the whole weight of your spirit into it. Okay, get ready. But wait. There's one thing I'm going to suggest that I know will help you.

6. Stand up. If you don't believe this helps, just try it. Standing releases a flow of energy that simply doesn't exist when you're sitting. Best of all, I actually like a wireless phone so I can do some

pacing. You know what? When I stand I feel I can lick the world. I can make that call. I'll get that visit. I'm standing and I'm determined. You'll feel exactly the same.

7. Smile when you talk. Your prospect will "hear" the smile in your voice. Explain that you're following up on the letter you sent and want to know when it might be convenient to meet.

8. Keep the small talk brief. Oh certainly, be cordial and pleasant. But your focus has to be on setting the visit.

"Hi, Mary. This is Jerry Panas. I sent you a letter the other day about the new library at Middleton School. When is a good time to see you and John, next Tuesday or Thursday?"

That may strike you as terse. Okay, do what's comfortable. But your task isn't to engage in extended conversation. Your job is to get the visit.

9. Be upfront about the amount of time you'll need. "I'd like an hour with you. Will that be all right?"

What happens if the prospect says she can only give you 20 minutes? "Well, I was hoping for more, but if you're tight on time, let's do it in 20 minutes. This program's so important I'm willing to take whatever time you've got." (You've probably found, as I have, that when a person tells you he can only give you 15 or 20 minutes, he ends up giving you all the time you need.)

10. Be focused. Your job is to set the date for the visit. It's not to make the sale or discuss the case. Don't fall into the trap of trying to make the sale on the phone. It won't work.

11. Move the conversation on and set the date. I like giving a person a choice of dates: "What's best for you, John, next Tuesday or next Thursday." Social psychologists tell us that a person is much more apt to make a positive decision if there's a choice.

•••

Great! You've got the date. You're well on your way to getting the gift. Follow this immediately with a letter of confirmation and appreciation. Make it brief (*Letter 4 in the Appendix*).

I never call to confirm a date before the visit. In fact, I try to make myself virtually unreachable! I don't want to make it convenient or easy for a person to cancel at the last minute. I let my letter put all the arrangements in place.

One last tip. Call your best prospects first, those you feel are the easiest to talk with. After a few calls, you'll have the model down pat.

9

THE SECRETS OF SUCCESS DON'T WORK UNLESS YOU DO

———■———

Let's set the scene. You've dialed the number. The prospect is on the phone. You've gone through the initial pleasantries. You have your calendar handy.

The moment has come. Your purpose is to set the date.

> **"John. You know how involved I am with The Salvation Army. I want to bring you up to date on some things we're doing. I'm certain you'll find it exciting. Is Tuesday or Wednesday of next week the better day for us to get together?"**

I wish it were easy, but often it's not. Be prepared. The one thing you can expect is the unexpected. Sometimes you run into a problem. Every winner has scars.

> "Jerry, I'm not sure it's a good idea to get together. I don't believe I want to get involved in the campaign. I contribute to the annual fund — I'm not interested in doing more."

You hoped for better, but didn't get it. You could leave it at that, thank the person for his consideration, and go on to the next prospect. But you know better. You know it's going to take a personal visit to get the gift you want. And you know your cause is so important, and so many lives are involved, that you have to exert yourself. This isn't easy. You'd prefer having your teeth scraped, but you go on.

> "It's important I see you, John. The choice to be involved is entirely yours. I'm not smart enough to persuade you to do something you don't want. But this program is the most important thing we can be doing in our community. All I'm asking is a chance to invite you into the partnership with us. I understand there may be personal circumstances. But you know me well enough to know you can be honest and I'll respect whatever you decide. What time is better for you next week, Tuesday or Wednesday?"

There, you did it. It wasn't easy, but you did it.

> "Jerry, just tell me how much you're looking for. Maybe we can do this on the phone. I really don't have much time. And I'm not crazy about fundraising and being asked."

This isn't getting any easier. What's the old Chinese torture -- having your toenails pulled? I think I'd prefer that. But I won't give up. Not yet.

> "I just don't feel comfortable trying to handle this on the phone. It's too important. Look, I'm willing to give it 30 minutes if you can give me that much time, too. Will you do that for me? Will you give me 30 minutes? What's going to be better for you, Tuesday or Wednesday? We can get over the business quickly and then go on to lunch."

What happens if you're still swimming upstream and the tide's against you? Your prospect says:

> "Look, why don't you just send me all of the information. I promise to look it over and I'll send you a check."

You know that would be the worst of options. Take one more shot.

> "Knowing you as I do, I really believe you'd give it a careful reading and send a check. And that would be important to us and to me personally. But, the material simply can't convey the importance and excitement of this program. I really believe it's something that will interest you. I know how busy you are, but I'm willing to match my time with yours. When can I come to see you? Next Tuesday or Wednesday?"

Every time I call for a visit, I think of a couple of lines from *Waiting for Godot*. They keep running through my mind. Estragon says: "I can't go on like this." Vladimir replies: "That's what you think."

These are just a few of the stiff-arms you can get. They're legitimate. I don't even call them objections. They're the kind of responses you should expect.

Here are a few more:

> "Jerry, I already give so much. You know I've been giving to them for years."

> "John, I know that. In fact, that's one of the reasons I'm calling on you. You've been such a great friend to us over the years. It's our friends we're calling on now for this program."

Keep in mind, your job is to get the visit, not to make the case, as much as your prospect may try to corner you into doing so.

> "Listen, Jerry, why don't you tell me what this is all about. We could probably do a lot of this on the phone. Tell me about the program."

> "It's a great project, John. The truth is, I couldn't do it justice on the phone. I have a feeling this is something you're going to be interested in, and I have some photographs and material I want to share with you. You're going to find this important. When is a good time to meet you next week, Tuesday or Wednesday?"

And, keep in mind, you're not to solicit on the telephone -- as much as your prospect may try to move you in that direction.

> "We're both so busy, Jerry. I know you're coming to talk with me about a gift but I think we can handle this on the phone -- and save some time. Just tell me about it now."

"I know this is something that's going to interest you, John, and that's why I'm so keen on seeing you. I don't feel I can do it justice on the phone, and I think we'd both lose if I tried. I know how busy you are. The folks I'm calling on are all terribly busy and that's why I'm careful about the time I take for a visit. I'm sure we can wrap this all up in 30 minutes. I'm hoping you'll give me that much time. I'm not smart enough to talk you into a gift but I do want to see you. When is a good day for a visit next week, Tuesday or Wednesday?"

If all else fails, here's one last suggestion I offer volunteers. It gets wonderful results. They tell me it almost always turns the prospect around. Use it only as your last resort.

"I know how busy you are, John. That's one of the reasons I'm eager to see you. You're the kind of person who gets things done. The truth is, I really didn't want to take on this assignment. I don't like fundraising. It's not something I look forward to. I said I'd do it because this program is so darn important. When Stanley, the chairman of the campaign, finally got me to take this on, I promised I'd call on all of those I was assigned to. I made that commitment. And you're one of the important ones I feel I really must see."

Try it. You're going to find this works.

10

No One Ever Listened Himself Out of a Gift

———■———

I may be one of the few who likes shopping for a car. I enjoy hearing about all the good stuff -- the carburetor, the compression ratio, the manifold. I even ask about the length of the axle. I don't know what any of it means. I just like to see how the various showroom salespeople handle themselves.

Well, Felicity and I were shopping for a new car recently. We walked into the showroom and began looking at one of the first cars in our path.

In no time a salesman came up, introduced himself, and began singing the virtues of the car we were perusing. We had a 20-minute discourse on gas consumption, safety features, and motor efficiency.

Here's what I found interesting. Not once did

he stop to ask us any questions. Not a single question. He had absolutely no idea what we might be interested in.

Soon, we moved on to another showroom not far away.

We were greeted at the door by a salesperson. She spent the first 15 or 20 minutes peppering us with questions. She wanted to know about our needs, the size of the family, what we had in mind, the amount and type of traveling we did, and whether this would be our primary car or a second car.

By the time she finished, she seemed to know precisely the car we wanted. No surprise! And we bought it.

Most prospects won't really listen or pay attention to what you're trying to sell until they're absolutely convinced you've heard and appreciated their point of view. As Montaigne said, what a person wants most in life is to be heard.

Here's the problem in fundraising when you talk instead of listen:

• You don't learn anything about the prospect, his needs and desires.

• You won't hear any concerns because you're not probing.

• You won't uncover any giving-clues.

• Your prospect is more apt to "buy" when he's talking than when you're talking.

• You won't understand what she's willing to invest in.

- You may raise negative issues the prospect hadn't thought of.
- You don't allow the prospect to gain owner-ship. There's no process for empowerment.
- You never have to regret what you don't say.
- You provide more opportunity for your prospect to disagree with you on some of your statements.
- You dominate the conversation instead of guiding it.
- You don't put the spotlight on the prospect and give her center stage.
- You don't give yourself breathing time to think ahead.

Note this well. In order to "listen the gift," you talk during the presentation for 25 percent of the time and the prospect talks for the balance. It's the most effective way to be on the same wavelength with the prospect and make him feel you've really listened.

Make it a give-and-take process. But as far as you're concerned, it's mostly take. I'm convinced that effective fundraisers don't sell the gift. They "listen the gift."

If you listen carefully enough, empathetically, you'll know precisely the prospect's needs and greatest passions. You'll learn what size of gift to ask for and what will motivate the person to make that gift.

11

DONORS GIVE TO THE MAGIC OF AN IDEA

---■---

People don't give because your organization has needs. Thousands of organizations have overwhelming financial problems (and opportunities). There's a facility to be renovated, equipment to be purchased, a roof in need of repair, additional staff for a necessary program.

But your donors run away from "needs." They hide from the institution that isn't financially stable. Major donors give to bold, heroic, and audacious programs rather than to needy institutions.

Keep in mind, too, that your organization doesn't have needs. People have needs. Your organization has the answer, the solution to problems and challenges. Don't sell needs -- sell your answer, your response, your successful solutions.

What, then, are the most important factors in motivating a person to make a major gift?

First and foremost is a belief in the mission of the institution. The person has to be closely aligned to the organization's vision, programs and objectives.

In the studies I've done, two factors are tied for second in importance in prompting a person to give. Both are significant, but far beneath a "belief in the mission of the institution."

One is: "The financial stability of the institution." No one wants to save the sinking Titanic! That's why you don't want to talk about your organization's needs.

Tied with financial stability is "a belief and regard for a staff person," usually the CEO. And that explains why it's so helpful to take a staff person when making your call.

What's not important, we learned, is the campaign material. I'm reminded that the shelf life of the average four-color, blind-embossed brochure is somewhere between milk and yogurt. Oh certainly, you need material, but don't be waving it around or pulling it out immediately. You'll break the spell.

Your prospect will be much more attentive to your oral presentation. Speak the magic and the vision. Then at an appropriate time, show the drawing of the new building or a photo of a group of youngsters in the swimming pool.

In studies we've conducted, it's always the oral presentation that motivates the gift. In fact, most prospects can't remember the printed material. And don't depend on a fancy audio-visual or PowerPoint presentation to get the gift.

Typically, I don't bring out the campaign material until the very end. And there are times when I don't even do that.

12

THE ARCHER STRIKES THE TARGET, PARTLY BY PULLING, PARTLY BY LETTING GO

———■———

You sent the letter. You made the phone call. You set the date. In some ways, it really wasn't as difficult as you thought, even though the phone call didn't follow your script exactly.

You're now 85 percent on your way to getting the gift.

Then, faster than you hoped, the day arrives and you're in the home or office of your prospect.

The first order of business, of course, is to establish a rapport and common ground. There's no magic to how long this should take. Take whatever time is necessary. Just be sure that small talk doesn't dominate your session and steal from your clear mission -- to get the gift.

Still, no matter how winsome you are, your prospect knows you're not there on a social call or an inquiry about his health. He's thinking: "What's she going to ask me for?" Or, "What do you suppose she has me down for?" Or, "I wonder where they got my name?" Or "Why the devil did I agree to this visit?"

That's what's going through his head. He's not hearing a word you're saying.

I know it's true. I've learned it in study after study we've conducted.

Here's what I suggest. You needn't use my words. Find your own rhythm and what works best for you and turns your words into music.

I called on Jim recently. He loves his university and went there on a scholarship. I began my visit this way.

> **"I've come today to talk with you about the University and its vision for the future. There's a project in particular I want to discuss — it's something I think you'll be interested in. (Pause) I'm not going to ask you for a gift today. I want to make that clear. We're not even going to discuss money. I just want to tell you about this project. But I'll be coming back and when I do, I'm going to ask you for a great deal of money. But not today."**

Being clear at the outset that you're not going to ask for money on this visit overcomes immense emotional blocks and hurdles. I've put his mind at ease.

Jim actually began listening to me then. He took his hands out of his pockets. He no longer clutched his wallet.

As I talked about the program, I discovered that Jim was finding part of it irresistible.

I asked open questions: "Jim, how do you feel about this program?" I probed. I listened. I tested for concerns.

We had a thorough discussion. And Jim had plenty of opportunity to ask his own questions. Finally I got to that point where I'd normally ask for a gift. Instead, I did something pretty much like this.

> **"It's been wonderful having the time with you. And I can see you're interested in the program. I was certain you would be. Pull out your calendar. I want to set a time for another visit."**

Almost always, the person will say: "Aw, come on -- there's no need to set another date. We can talk about the money today. It's okay. I know you have something in mind." That's almost exactly what Jim did say.

My response:

> **"The truth is, Jim, I'm not smart enough to know how much you should give. That's really your decision. But for a program like this, I thought you'd want to make a gift of $1 million."**

Note, I didn't say he *should* make a gift of $1 million. I said I was pretty sure he would want to make a gift of that size. Note my words. I chose them carefully.

"I thought you would want...."

I haven't even asked for a gift. I've merely mentioned what I feel Jim would want to do for a program of this importance and interest.

We negotiated and talked some more and he raised some valid concerns. In the end, it did take another visit -- but I knew I was well on my way to getting that gift. And I did!

13

YOU'LL NEVER KNOW IF YOU DON'T ASK

———■———

I find my early minutes with prospects are often my most valuable. It's not idle chatter. I'm actually on a fact-finding mission.

How did they happen to go to the University? How was the experience?

How are their youngsters doing at the School? How do you feel about the School?

How important is an organization like the YMCA in our community?

How do you feel about their work and service?

Note these are all open questions. While you're uncovering valuable information, you're building rapport. And you'll find that the more time you take in seeking rapport, the less it will appear later that you're using pressure.

If you're talking to a prospect and you're not quite sure how great his interest is (and often this will be the case), you need to fully explore the situation.

"We've talked a little bit about the YMCA and the impact it's making in our community. I told you about some of their programs where they're touching the lives of young people in a way no other organization does. It seemed to me that you're concerned about the need for work in the inner-city. How important do you feel this is? How do you feel about the role of the YMCA and what they're doing?"

It is essential that you probe for concerns. Often what you don't like to hear is exactly what you should listen to most.

Use open questions – and listen. If you spend all of your time talking, you'll uncover no new information. If you never walk except where there are tracks, you'll never make new discoveries.

I remember several years ago when I was making a call with a volunteer for a major campaign for the hospital in Salisbury, Maryland. We had scripted it well and the volunteer, Fulton Jeffers, knew he was to probe and ask.

Fulton began the call by asking the prospect how he felt about the hospital. The response was startling: "It's a horrible place. I think the medical staff stinks. The nursing care is terrible. When I was in there, they didn't have anyone on the floor who spoke English. The place is filthy."

I was thinking of the Cheyenne warrior battle cry: It's a good day to die.

Fulton was quick: "Ben, I am embarrassed. I thought I knew you so well. I felt you loved the hospital and would be interested in this program. I'm obviously wrong. Tell me more about what happened so we can get to the bottom of this."

Ben went on, nonstop, for the next fifteen or twenty minutes. He finally wound down. And then something very special happened. When he got it all out of his system, he seemed to feel much better.

Finally he said: "Well, maybe it wasn't as bad as I've made out. And we certainly need a good hospital in Salisbury. What did you want to talk with me about?"

We went on to get the gift.

I was reminded of the spiritual axiom that God never closes one door without opening another. But sometimes the hallway in between is murder.

The secret was Fulton's thoughtful way of handling the complaint and his ability to listen with interest and concern. He tuned out the world and tuned Ben in.

Work hard at putting people completely at ease and making them feel important. Get them talking about themselves and their concerns. Probe. Hold eye contact and listen to how they feel. Understand fully that people are more likely to listen to you later if you listen to them first.

14

CONSISTENT HARD WORK IS THE YEAST THAT RAISES THE DOUGH

———■———

I know what it's like. I can give personal testimony.

When I first started calling on folks for a gift, I was terrified. That's the truth of it. I could easily get through the early stages of the presentation, and talk with ease about the programs and the needs of those served.

But when it came to that frightening moment when I was to ask for a gift, I froze. I felt like I had a chicken bone caught in my throat. All of a sudden I understood the song, *"Bewitched, Bothered, and Bewildered."*

I've had successful Fortune 500 executives tell

me the same. They suffer the butterflies of the Gladiator squinting at the Emperor's box for a thumbs-up or a thumbs-down.

I've talked with successful business leaders, college presidents, and multimillionaires who can achieve just about anything in life -- except to ask for a gift. Even highly productive life insurance salespeople feel the same agony. It's what John Steinbeck described as "the urge to be someplace else."

I've heard it all, and have felt some of it myself:

"I'm afraid that the person I call on will say no."

"When I get ready to ask, I get all choked up."

"I hate to beg." (You're not begging, by the way. You're inviting a person to join with others in a noble cause -- a program that will change lives and save lives. If you're begging, you won't get the gift.)

Still another person told me he can't stand rejection.

But you'll never know unless you ask. The single overriding reason people indicate why they haven't made a gift is -- you've guessed it -- they weren't asked.

A monk asks a superior if it is permissible to smoke while praying. The superior responds with a quick rebuke: "Absolutely not."

The next day the monk asks the superior if it's acceptable to pray while smoking. "That is not only permissible," says the superior, "it is admirable."

See, you never know unless you ask.

Step back and consider what happens if you

do get no for an answer. I've learned it's not the solicitor who's being turned down. In almost all cases, it means there isn't a meshing of the prospect's passions and interests with the mission of the institution.

There's nothing you could have done about that. People give for their reasons, not yours. It's their loss. Go on to the next prospect.

I tell my solicitors that they're not smart enough to talk a reluctant donor into a gift. And they shouldn't even try. Go on to the next. There's a whole world waiting to give to you.

What's clear to me is that there's no permanent damage to the solicitor who is turned down. You can survive. The important thing is to ask.

Even if you didn't get the gift, your spouse and friends love you. The dog greets you at the door and wags his tail and wets all over your shoes with joy. Life is good.

And one more thing of importance. If you're not getting rejections, it probably means you're not getting many acceptances either. You can't be in the wonderful game of asking for gifts without expecting some disappointments.

Wayne Gretzky, the great hockey all-time scorer, said: "One hundred percent of the shots I never take don't go in."

15

A SUCCESSFUL FUNDRAISER SHOOTS AT A TARGET NO ONE ELSE SEES, AND HITS IT

———■———

You've come to that point in the visit when you must present the magic of your cause -- the challenge, the drama, the need, the urgency. Take no more than eleven minutes. Take less time if possible.

Let me explain the eleven minutes.

Oh, sure, you can take more if necessary. But not much. And at your own risk! All the research indicates this is about the maximum time a person can handle without tuning you out.

I'll give you an analogy that confirms my conviction. When you plan a video, the producer will tell you it mustn't be any longer than eight to twelve minutes. Some say five. There's good reason for that. A video of this kind won't hold a person's attention for any longer.

Which is surprising since the video has a great deal going for it. There's a musical background, professional narration, even sound effects. Heck, it's like a gypsy wedding going on in the background.

And with all this, it still should be limited to eight to twelve minutes. So, if your dazzling presentation can be that inspiring, you may take more time -- but be forewarned.

All right, so you're ready for your presentation. Here are a few tips that will be helpful.

1. When you discuss the opportunity with the prospect, it's not enough to talk about how the gift will benefit the institution and those served. It is essential to convey the benefits to the actual donor.

Discuss how many lives this program will change. Discuss the joy the gift will bring to the donor, the recognition, and the sense that he is indeed directly saving lives.

To get the largest gift possible, it has to be a win-win situation -- for the institution and the donor.

2. Be careful not to make the size of the gift dominate the presentation. Make it secondary to determining what most effectively fills the needs of the prospect.

You're not trying to manipulate the donor. Tricky

negotiations, fast-talking, and smart gimmicks are all repugnant.

Instead, understand full well that you're helping the prospect to make an investment that will bring joy and satisfaction. The purpose of the gift is to help solve a pressing and urgent problem.

Don't sell the institution. Talk about the return on investment.

3. The case for your program must have relevancy, drama, and emotional appeal. But most of all, there must be a great sense of urgency.

The stakes are high, time is pressing, lives will suffer or may be lost. The need is overwhelming and the solution you propose is the effective answer. Now is the time to respond.

4. Shy away from talking about big, abstract numbers. The fact that you have an all-time high of 11,000 students isn't very dramatic. Or that you served 50,000 in the emergency room -- that's not very compelling. Nor that there are 3,000 homeless in the streets of our city.

I like to think of what I call The Anne Frank Concept. It's hard to comprehend and identify with three million children who died in the Holocaust. But it's easy to get overwhelmed with the Anne Frank story. When making a presentation, think Anne Frank.

5. Along the way, remember to have fun. Keep in mind Maya Angelou's comment, no matter what happens: "You knew what you knew how to do, and when you knew better, you did better."

People don't care how much you know until they know how much you care. Bring your passion, commitment, and joy to your calls. People take heart when you give them yours.

16

SOME AIM AT NOTHING & HIT IT WITH REMARKABLE PRECISION

———■———

I did it wrong for years, and wondered why I didn't have better results. (They say stupidity is doing the same thing in the same way, but expecting different results.)

When the time finally comes to ask for the gift, you ask for a specific amount.

Let's say you're at that special point in the discussion when you're ready to ask. "I'd like you to consider a gift of $10,000 to $25,000," you say. That's the way I did it for years -- and the truth is, I was just plain happy to get the amount out of my mouth without gagging.

But what happens when you give a range?

The floor becomes the ceiling. The request I just cited will turn into a gift of $10,000 ... or nothing. And here's why.

First, it's much easier to give $10,000 than $25,000. And if that amount seems satisfactory to the asker, "So be it" says the donor.

But, second, when you give a range, it signifies you don't know much about the donor. "She doesn't know anything about me," thinks the prospect, "none of my desires and personal needs. She probably doesn't have any idea of what I give to other institutions or what I think of her cause. She's just throwing some amounts on the wall, hoping one will stick."

Well, then, how much should you ask for? It's a tough question. And one of the most important you'll face.

Your institution has likely given you a figure to suggest to your prospect. I'm going to give you some general guidelines, too. Think of them only as yardsticks. They'll get you within yards of what you need to know, but not inches. The inches part of it is based partly on your good intuition and what you learn from your probing and questioning during the session.

Here are some general guidelines.

1. Liquidity is the key. The donor has to have funds that can be made available for your program.

2. Real estate and agriculture can often mean: Land rich, cash poor. If all of the prospect's assets are tied up in real estate, you'll likely have a difficult time unless he's planning a gift of property.

3. Valuable property is expensive to maintain. I've stopped trying to determine the size of the gift based on the value of the home and second property. Some of these folks have mortgages up to their kazoo and are spending a great deal to maintain the expensive property.

4. Annual gifts generally come from income, major and capital gifts come from assets. Typically, if you're looking for a significant gift to a capital project, it won't come out of annual income (*see Appendix D*).

5. Consider the age, number of children, family obligations (second marriage?), healthcare situations, those kind of variables.

6. A major gift equals 10 to 25 times consistent annual giving. If the annual gift is $10,000, the specific gift you should ask will end up being somewhere in the range of $100,000 to $250,000.

7. Still, despite all of the figures and careful projections, nothing (nothing!) takes the place of the person's attitude toward philanthropy, her interest in the mission of your organization, and her involvement in the institution.

Giving is based on the need-fulfillment of the donor. This has overriding importance and can move a gift many degrees one way or the other.

17

THE LINE BETWEEN SUCCESS & FAILURE: 'I DIDN'T MAKE MY OWN GIFT FIRST'

—■—

You've set the stage and done a superb job! As correct as a finger bowl. You began with a positive attitude, you probed and asked open questions, and you listened.

Now comes one of the most telling and effective parts of the presentation. I want you, the volunteer, to give testimony to your own gift.

This is a good point to remind you of an immutable rule -- never make a call unless you've made your own gift first.

This seems obvious but it's worth repeating because it's so important. Why should anyone else give if you don't care enough to make your own gift?

When I talk with volunteers about making a gift, I ask them to consider a sacrificial gift. But for some, that may seem too daunting. Let's just say that I want the volunteer to give at a level that makes him stand on tiptoes.

Buddha called it Dharma -- the phenomenon that only when you give with your heart are you able to open yourself to receive.

I remember a call I made early in my career. I was with a volunteer, and she had made a superb presentation. When she finished and asked for the gift, the prospect said: "This seems like something I'd be interested in. How much have you given to the project?"

That's a fair question. I can assure you that even if it isn't asked, it's something the prospect would like to know. It's one way of gauging the appropriateness of the ask.

In this case, the solicitor said: "Well ... my husband and I haven't made up our minds yet. We're still thinking about it."

The prospect was plenty upset. "Why don't we just finish this off now," he said tersely. "And when you make up your mind and decide what you're going to give, come back and see me."

I'll never make that mistake again.

Here's an example of how you might give testimony to your gift:

"I'm going to ask you, John, to share with me in this program. But before I do, let me tell

you what Felicity and I decided to give. We're giving $50,000. You know us pretty well and you know that'll really stretch us. It's the largest gift we've ever made to anything. We thought about it for a long time, we discussed it, and we even prayed about it. We decided that this program was so important ...."

Giving "testimony" is important because it provides credence to your own commitment and faith in the program.

It does something else too. It takes all you've said about the institution and its vision, and positioned it in terms of its personal impact on you. It's what Theodore Roosevelt called: "Giving unambiguous demonstration of where I firmly stand."

18

TRIUMPH IS
JUST 'UMPH'
ADDED TO TRY

—■—

Now you've come to the moment of truth --
when you must ask for the gift. You've done a great
job. You probed. You asked questions. You listened.
You presented a dramatic and urgent opportunity.
And you gave testimony to your own gift.

Everything you've done has led to this moment.
There's suspense. Plenty. But that's okay. We all feel
it. I still do when I'm ready to ask for a gift.

The tenseness in the room crackles. It's raining
stress and strain. The heartbeat quickens.

And your prospect feels the same pangs of angst,
too. There's so much excitation between the two
of you, you feel like one of the brothers in *Beau
Geste*, the classic film about the French Foreign
Legion, where they touch each other to see if

they're still alive.

And finally you're ready to transform your entire visit into the invitation to give. The words I use are fairly simple:

"I would like you to consider a gift of..."

That's how easy it is. Not much magic to all of that. Simply: "I would like you to consider a gift of ...."

Those are the words that work most effectively for me. But find whatever feels best and most comfortable for you. Find the words to your own song. For instance, "I would like to invite you to join us ...."

You've asked for the gift. You wait. The moment is suddenly flooded with silence, a thundering quiet.

The next point is very important. *Do not fill in the silence.*

Wait for the prospect to speak. It will seem like hours. There are times I felt the silence was so painfully long I could be excused to go for a walk. Or do hand puppets!

You want to break the silence, to say anything: "Have you noticed there will be a full moon tomorrow!"

But resist the temptation -- don't talk. If you do, you may never know how the prospect really feels about the program and the gift. The secret of success, I've learned, is holding on for a minute longer.

19

AN OBSTACLE IS WHAT YOU SEE WHEN YOU TAKE YOUR EYES OFF THE OBJECTIVE

———■———

You've gone through your presentation. You established an effective foundation by probing and asking questions. You encouraged your prospect to do most of the talking.

You felt during the entire time that there was great endorsement of the organization. You were encouraged because the prospect seemed intent, raised appropriate questions, and nodded approvingly throughout.

Everything was properly in place.

You came to those simple words that transform your entire visit into an invitation for a gift: "I would like you to consider a gift of ...." You asked for a specific amount and then you paused.

The response was not entirely surprising.

"I'm not really certain, Jerry. It's something I'll need to think over."

Good!

Yes, good! You couldn't have hoped for a better response -- unless it was something like: "As a matter of fact Jerry, I'm going to give three times as much as you asked for." (Oh sure! I've been waiting for that to happen.)

You now have an opportunity to learn how the prospect really feels about your program and the request. You don't know that yet and you mustn't go on until you do. You are ready to ask the *Four Magic Questions*. That's all there are, just four.

My typical reply to the prospect's response would be something like this:

"Of course, Mary, you're going to need more time to think this over. I've suggested a significant gift. But let me ask you..."

I will then proceed to ask Mary the *Four Magic Questions* to determine the reason for her hesitancy:

1. *Is it the institution?*
2. *Is it the project?*
3. *Is it the amount I asked for?*
4. *Is it the timing?*

Before I leave, I have to know how she feels about these issues. And so I probe.

"As we were talking, you seemed to indicate a great interest and support for our school.
Am I right about that?" (Is it the Institution?)

Mary says something like:

"Yes, I think it's a wonderful school."

Great! I got through the first question.

"The more we talked, the more I felt that
you were keenly interested in the Library. That
it's something dear to your heart." (Is it the
project?)

"You're absolutely right. I think the
Library's the most important thing our school
could undertake now."

Phew. We're through the second question. And
things are going quite well. I'm reciting psalms!

"I suggested you might want to consider a
gift of $50,000. I thought that was about the
amount you'd want to give to a program like
this. Am I correct about that?" (Is it the
amount?)

"That sounds about right although it may
be a little higher than I thought."

That's okay. I consider that a positive response.
I'm in the right ballpark on the amount. I'm getting close. There's only one last question.

"Mary, you feel so keenly about this program, perhaps it's the timing that's causing you
some concern. If you had an additional year or
two to complete your payments, would that
enable you to make the $50,000 gift you seem

to want to make?" (Is it the timing?)

"As a matter of fact, I do have some obligations I wasn't expecting yet...."

You see what I did, and what you need to do. The initial response from Mary didn't lead us anywhere. It was certainly better than a flat-out no, but it didn't give any indication if there were issues still needing to be resolved. In Mary's case, it was simply a matter of timing -- and that was an easy one to adjust.

You need to know the answers to these *Four Magic Questions*. Even if I get a no, I ask the same questions (the only dumb questions are the ones you don't ask).

I once asked Stanley Marcus how he felt when someone said no to his request for a gift. Stanley was former CEO of famed Neiman Marcus for years and one of the greatest salesmen of the last century. He said: "I never take no for an answer. Even if the person dies, I consider it only a maybe!"

20

OBJECTIONS AREN'T BITTER IF YOU DON'T SWALLOW THEM

———■———

Confession is good for the soul. I must admit when I first started in fundraising, I hated objections. I felt like the tin man cowering before the Wizard of Oz.

There I was, just finishing a flawless and dazzling presentation. And I could just see my prospect winding up, ready to deliver a whammo objection. I wanted to run for cover. What do you do when you stand at the crossroads and all of the signposts are gone?

But what I realize now is that objections are indeed your best friends. They're often the way prospects mask their concerns for help and more information.

I now encourage objections. I do! I probe for hidden or unspoken ones.

Here's what I know. A gift at the proper level won't be made until every concern, no matter how inappropriate or trivial, is satisfied.

The objections may feel like a personal assault, perhaps even an attack. But they're not. Your first impulse is to be defensive, to strike back. But don't.

Remember, your job isn't to prevail, knock down, and win. Your job is to resolve the objection and win over the prospect.

I like the story of the foreman who was very hardworking and conscientious. But he hadn't received a promotion in ten years. Asked if he had an explanation for his failure to advance, he replied: "Many years ago, I had an argument with my supervisor. I won."

Your success will depend on your ability to go from one objection to another without loss of your optimism or enthusiasm.

Probe some more, ask questions, get deeper into the concern. Remain poised, interested, completely understanding, confident, and positive. Just do what it says on the back of the Hellman's Mayonnaise jar: Keep cool and don't freeze!

For me, objections were the worst part of the call. But what I finally learned is that objections are like a grindstone. They either grind you down or polish you up. What happens depends on you.

If you don't respond to all possible objections, you're not going to get the gift at the level you want.

21

GREAT OPPORTUNITY STANDS BESIDE YOU, IN THE FORM OF OBJECTIONS

———————■———————

I'm going to give you some typical objections you may encounter and the sort of response I would give. I'll use a hospital for my example, but the objections will be pretty much the same no matter the institution.

In this chapter, I'll also give you a formula I often use. It's quite simple: *Feel, Felt, Found.* I think you'll find it extremely helpful.

Feel indicates clearly that you really have listened to the person's objection. *Felt* signals that you can empathize with their situation. *Found* demonstrates that there is a happy solution.

It really works.

One word of caution. I wouldn't use this approach more than twice in a session with a person, three times at the most. After awhile, your prospects will say: No more of that *feel, felt, found* business. I understand what you're doing!

Here are three examples (*you'll find more in Appendix B*):

OBJECTION: *I can't make a decision now. I'll have to talk it over with . . .*

RESPONSE: I'm not surprised at all. I suspect you and I have been talking about a gift larger than you anticipated. Take your time to think it over and talk with your husband. And perhaps even your accountant. Let's set a time now that I might be able to see you and your husband together. I want to be able to tell him about this program and perhaps it'll be easier for me to convey the urgency. When is a good time to see you next?

• *Or, Feel, Felt, Found*

I know how you *feel* about making a decision on the spot. As a matter of fact, I hate to be pinned down like that myself. That's why, when they asked me to make my gift, I *felt* exactly like you. I wanted more time, I wanted an opportunity to review it with my wife, and perhaps check with my accountant to see what would be the best timing. I *found* that a small delay was helpful and it meant I didn't get carried away with the excitement of hearing about the program and acting immediately.

But I knew there was a timeline that the folks at the Hospital were working under so I promised I'd make a decision within a week. Heck, for most people, it doesn't take longer than that. When's a good time to come see you again? How about in two weeks?

OBJECTION: *Leave the material and the Letter of Intent with me. I'll look it over and then mail in my gift.*

RESPONSE: There's no question in my mind you would. And I'm so pleased you're showing an interest in supporting the program. But this campaign is so important to me -- and I hope to you -- that I want to be present to discuss the next step with you. I made a commitment I'd do everything I could to personally follow through. That's why I want to be certain to talk with you once more about the Letter of Intent. When's a good time to see you again? Can you pull out your calendar? Can we get back together in about two weeks?

• *Or, Feel, Felt, Found*

I know how you *feel*. I *felt* I might be pressed into signing something I wouldn't be happy with afterwards. That's why I asked for another week or so to think it over. The person who called on me explained how important it was to pick up the Letter of Intent in person and review once more any questions I still had.

Don't worry, I'm not going to try to talk you into a larger gift -- I'm not smart enough to do that. I *found* that the second visit was actually very helpful. I still had a few questions I needed answers for, and I got them in that session.

And as it turned out, we made some special arrangements for the way this would be paid out that worked to my advantage. I really wouldn't have known about all of this if we hadn't had that second visit. Take out your calendar and let's look at a date when we can get together again. How about in two weeks?

OBJECTION: *This is a terrible time to ask me for a gift. I've got a daughter's wedding and a kid going through college.*

RESPONSE: I know what you're going through. I've been there myself. You can get pretty stretched out, can't you? I think the important thing for us to discuss is how you feel about the hospital program and what you'd be inclined to do if you didn't have these extra expenses right now.

If you feel as concerned about the hospital as I believe you do, it'll be easy to work out the timing so you don't have to make the first payment for another couple of years.

The important thing for the success of this campaign and what we need to know now is what you intend to do. Let's talk for a moment about what you would like to do if you didn't have those expenses now.

• *Or, Feel, Felt, Found*

I know how you *feel*, I certainly do. You feel like some of those costs and the tuition will never end. Thankfully, they do. There are a lot of folks who *felt* the same way you did and so here's what we've arranged.

We *found* that what's most important to keep the momentum going is to determine what friends like you would like to give when you have fewer of these unusual expenses. Just let me know what you would intend to do and I'll be able to report that.

It's not legally binding. It's only your intention of what you'd like to do. Just being able to add to our totals give encouragement to everyone.

•••

Objections are tough. But it's essential you probe to find out if there are any problems. In Schubert's *Der Hirt Auf Dem Felsen*, he writes: "I am consumed with grief. My joy is at an end. Hope has deserted me." I know the feeling!

But believe me, objections are your friends because they will lead you to the gift.

**Note: See APPENDIX B for more
objections and responses.**

22

A DESK IS A DANGEROUS PLACE TO RAISE MONEY FROM

---■---

"Where am I?"

"In the hall."

"Where do I want to be?"

"In that man's office."

"What will happen if I go inside?"

"The worst is I'd be thrown back down the hall."

"Well, that's where I am now, so what have I got to lose?"

Have you ever had that conversation with yourself? I have. I know what it's like to have the dreaded disease -- *doorknobaphobia*.

The first few calls I made were horrifying. It was like opening a vein. That's because I had no idea of what to do.

I can still remember the first gift I ever received. I felt I was getting close. It had gone wonderfully well, everything according to script. I was at that special moment -- when it was time to ask.

I wanted to say: Make the gift and once it's committed, signed, notarized, and entered at the County Courthouse, I'll give you back the keys to your car! But I didn't. I asked properly and received the gift. And to my delight, the donor was as pleased as I was.

I learned what glorious fun and how important this could be, this mission of raising funds. I realized that through my efforts I was actually helping to change lives and save lives.

I was helping to build endowments, provide scholarships, send kids to camp, buy needed equipment, build new swimming pools, and libraries, and hospitals. Heck, I was as important in conquering cancer as the great scientist in the lab. Because if it weren't for me, there wouldn't be the funds for research.

I was making it happen. You're going to have this same feeling, too.

Me, I have a fantasy. I'm at those beautiful pearly gates. St. Peter is looking down at me. There's a long questionnaire in his hands. "And what did you do that we should let you in?" he says in a deep baritone.

I tell St. Peter I've been raising money for vital causes. I'm a crusader for important organizations.

A smile crosses his face. "Come in," he says, "we've been expecting you."

Lucky you. You are a fundraiser. Some shy away. Some are afraid. Some say they don't like it. You know better. You are, in your own special way, helping change a corner of the world.

23

IT'S AMAZING
WHAT YOU DON'T
RAISE WHEN YOU
DON'T ASK

---■---

If you didn't get the gift – and in some instances you won't -- there are usually ten "horrid reasons." There may be more, but these are the primary ones.

You may find that it'll take a call or two before you're able to avoid them all. I know in my own solicitations, my immediate instinct was to pull the shades, and devote the rest of my life to reading the collected works of Emily Dickinson.

But I soon learned that the mark of a successful and motivated fundraiser is the ability to distinguish a temporary setback from a defeat. I've been blessed with an invincible spirit (you will be, too, if you stick with it).

It's not a matter of whether you get knocked down. You do. It's whether you get up again. And I do. Giving up is the ultimate tragedy. Failure is not the crime -- low aspirations are.

Here are the ten "Horrid Reasons" to avoid.

1. *Didn't make the call to set up the visit.*

You committed the most grievous act of all. You never telephoned to set up the visit. You kept putting it off. Then you stared at the phone. And you stared. You hoped it would ring so you wouldn't have to punch in the number. But it didn't ring. You gathered up your material and walked away. Coward!

2. *Inadequate Preparation.*

You didn't take time to prepare or to know your prospect. And you didn't practice. You thought you could wing it. You went dashing into the session thinking: "I'll make the call and get it over with." You got the kind of results you deserved. George Allen, one of history's greatest football coaches, says that winning can be defined as the science of being totally prepared.

3. *Anxiety.*

You were nervous, insecure, and uncomfortable. It wasn't an easy visit, and it showed.

Chances are, if you were properly prepared and had practiced, you could have overcome this. There's no reason to be nervous. You know what must be done. You know the drill.

Be at ease. There are those who simply won't

be interested in your great cause. That's okay, they have a different agenda. There's nothing you could have done to change their mind. Go on to the next prospect.

4. *Assuming Too Much.*

You called on someone who you felt knew a good bit more about the institution and the project than was actually the case. You jumped to the ask too soon because you assumed too much.

Or you called on someone who had been actively involved in the institution for a period of years. You took for granted she'd be interested in the project.

You felt no need to interpret, to sell the dream, to discuss how important her gift would be. That's what you thought! You asked for the gift too soon -- you leaped from step one to step nine. You lose.

5. *Failure to Probe.*

The prospect was nodding in approval, smiling and throwing off all the positive physical signs during your entire presentation. Even the body language seemed right. You left thinking you'd made the case, made the sale.

But you failed to probe for any concerns, determine whether there were lingering questions. You realize that George Bernard Shaw said it all in the title of his wonderful play, *You Never Can Tell*. You didn't ask the *Four Magic Questions*.

If you don't probe, you haven't even begun to make the ask.

6. *Poor Listening.*

You talked too much, you listened too little. You never found out how the prospect felt about the program because you spent all of your time talking. You failed to "listen the gift."

The more attentive you are in listening to others, the more likely they will listen to you. Give your undivided attention to the prospect.

The person asking the questions -- that's you -- is in control of the conversation. An attorney examining and probing a witness is a prime example. He questions, probes, examines, directs the interrogation and the content of what the judge and jury hear.

The person who listens influences the outcome, not the talker. You are in charge. Listen!

7. *Too Much on Features and Not Enough on Benefits.*

You spent your time going over details and speaking about features (the gymnasium will be regulation size, the new center will have nine Conference Rooms, the new Library can house 40,000 volumes). You pulled out the fancy brochure and reviewed the floor plans. But you failed to notice that the prospect's eyes had glazed over.

You spent too much time talking about money and not enough about the results and outcomes that could be expected from the prospect's investment.

The purpose of your presentation isn't to sell a program or a building. It's to help the prospect to visualize and enter into the world of the end result.

You didn't take enough time talking about how the program would save or change lives. You missed your golden opportunity.

8. *Premature Selling.*

You asked for the gift and made a brilliant close but you didn't take any of the necessary preliminary steps. You hadn't taken time to make the program properly irresistible. You hadn't probed for concerns or asked enough questions and taken time to listen.

You found the prospect nodding in agreement and you took that as a sign that you had finished the job. You raced from first to third base, without touching second.

9. *Win-Win.*

You spent all of your time talking about how important the program was for the institution and how it would meet its needs. You may have even shown the prospect a Gift Table and talked about the importance of major gifts (as if the prospect would make a sizable gift just because the institution needed it or the campaign would fail without it).

You didn't talk about those who would be served. More important, you didn't talk about how it would benefit the donor. You forgot your organization doesn't have needs. Those you serve have needs, and the gift you seek will help provide the solution.

10. *Didn't Ask.*

The most heinous sin of all -- you didn't ask.

You made a brilliant presentation, you asked all the right questions, you probed. You followed every step. It was a glorious session. One small omission -- you left before actually asking for the gift. You were so pleased with your performance, you forgot the last Act!

In my earlier days I was guilty of the same crime. Actually, in some cases, I was pleased to get out alive without having to make the dreaded ask. I could feel my tongue getting thick, my throat as dry as the Sahara.

If you wait for the perfect time, perfect conditions, the perfect opportunity when everything is just right (and the stars and the moon are in perfect alignment), you'll never ask.

Go ahead, ask for the gift. And take comfort in the fact that it's not the eloquence of your presentation which will determine your success or failure. It's the simple act of asking.

One thing is certain: if you don't ask, you won't get the gift.

24

YOU DON'T HAVE TO BE GREAT TO START, BUT YOU HAVE TO START TO BE GREAT

———■———

Here are the Golden Rules of Fundraising, the principles we've covered in the book. "Begin at the beginning," said the king bravely in Alice in Wonderland, "and go on till you come to the end. Then stop."

• Begin by knowing everything possible about the institution, its mission and vision for the future, its program, and the project.

• Make certain, in your heart-of-hearts, that you're completely committed to the worthiness of the institution and the significance and value of the project.

• Learn everything you can about the prospects you'll be calling on and their giving history.

• After careful assessment, determine the specific amount you should ask for.

• Give some thought as to how you'll express the amount of your request. Say it out loud several times before your visit.

• Eighty-five percent of getting the gift is setting up the visit. When doing so, don't make the case or try to get the gift on the telephone.

• Practice, practice, practice. Write out what you're going to say when you call for the visit.

• Write out in advance all of the reasons your prospect may try to put you off. Practice how to respond.

• When you make the visit, go in pairs.

• Call on your best prospects first.

• Remember what's most important to the donors you call on: *Empathy, Energy, and Enthusiasm.*

• During the visit, use your early moments to establish rapport. Take as much time as necessary. But remember, your objective is to talk about the project and to get the gift.

• It is essential that you probe for concerns.

• Ask open questions.

• Listen.

• Take no more than 11 minutes to present the project and its irrefutable rationale.

• The case for the project has to be relevant, have dramatic and emotional appeal, and provide a sense of urgency.

• Convey the benefit to the donor. It has to be a win-win for institution and the donor.

• Don't let the size of the gift dominate the presentation. It's all about mission -- not money.

• Don't sell features. Talk about outcomes and results.

• Give testimony to your own gift and what others have done.

• When finally making the ask, use words such as: "I would like you to consider a gift of...."

• Wait for a response. Don't fill in the silence -- no matter how long it seems to take.

• Don't let objections rattle you. They are your best friends. Probe for concerns. If you don't, you'll never know how the prospect really feels about the program.

• Use the *Four Magic Questions*: Is it the Institution? It is the Project? Is it the Amount? Is it the Timing?

• Get a commitment to something before leaving, either the gift or the date for another visit.

•••

And there you have it, the principles of success. You're going to be great. And if at first you do succeed, try not to show your astonishment!

25

IN ALL YOU DO, ACT AS IF IT'S IMPOSSIBLE TO FAIL

———■———

When all is said and done, here's how easy it is:

The Right Person
asks
The Right Prospect
for
The Right Amount
in
The Right Way
at
The Right Time
for
The Right Cause
with
The Right Follow-up.

And you ... you are the right person.

DEDICATION

This book is dedicated to the hundreds of thousands of volunteers and professionals involved in fundraising for great causes, toilers all in the vineyards of philanthropy. After the verb 'to love,' 'to help' is the most beautiful word in the language. You are helpers, all.

You are about to make your calls. Or you've made some already. Be prepared: You win some, you lose some. But no matter what the outcome, you are forever, to use Hemingway's salute: "The winner and still the undisputed champion."

Bless you one and all. Because of your toil and talent, you are saving lives and changing lives.

John R. Mott, one of the great Evangelists of the 1900s, said it well: "Blessed are the fundraisers, and in heaven they shall stand on the right hand of the martyrs."

That is just where you'll stand, too.

AN AFTERTHOUGHT

I've been meaning to do it for months.

I've wanted to ask Chester how successful he's been with fundraising. Just from watching him in action, he seems to be a very effective solicitor.

Let me tell you about Chester. He's an experienced professional fundraiser. That would be one way of putting it, a gentle way. Actually, well, he's a beggar. A street beggar.

Every night at six o'clock, he appears at the corner of 86th and Madison Avenue in New York, in front of the Food Emporium, one of city's more popular supermarkets.

He pulls out a wooden stool and sits on it. Rain or shine, every day, summer or winter, weekdays and weekends -- he appears on his stool. That's his corner, and I have a feeling no one would want to challenge Chester for his territory.

I live a block away and use that grocery store for my shopping. I've been there at all times in the evening, in all kinds of weather. He's always there. I don't know what time he leaves. I've wanted to ask him, and will someday, when I get to know him a little better.

He knows my name. I don't know how, but

that's the kind of guy he is. He seems to know the names of most of the regulars who pass. He's really good at what he does.

"Hi, Chester."

"Hi, Jerry."

I've been dying to ask him. So one day I get up the nerve. "Chester, you work this corner pretty well. How many people that walk by give to you?"

He tells me typically it's about one out of five. On a good day, about two out of five.

I want to ask Chester how much he makes on a good night. No, I'm not planning a career move. I'll stick to my own kind of fundraising. I'm just curious.

I'm telling you this story because if Chester can ask, with such success, so can you (and he doesn't have the advantage of prospect research, IT back-up, or solicitation coaching).

Because you represent such an important cause, you'll have a much higher percentage of success. Count on it!

And there's a vital point to remember -- you're not begging. Keep that in mind. You're asking men and women to join you in a noble cause, a pro-gram that represents compelling and urgent needs.

Because of you, through your great work, you will be directly helping change lives and save lives. You are the hero of this book.

By the way, if you're ever by the corner of 86th and Madison, stop and say hello to Chester. Let him know that among the "professional fundraisers" who work the streets of New York, he's one of the most famous. And drop in a few coins as a matter of professional courtesy.

APPENDIX

A. Letters

1. Staff makes the call for a joint visit
2. Volunteer letter to set-up a staff visit
3. Volunteer writes for a visit
4. Letter to confirm visit

B. More Objections & Responses

C. Profile of a Major Gift Donor and How Much to Ask for

D. Annual Giving vs. Major Gifts

Jean Smyth
345 Carey Street
Middleton, OH 97348

Dear Jim and Sally:

I've asked Sandra Guest to call in the next few days to set a time when we might visit you. As you well know, Sandra heads the development program for Middleton School and is a remarkable person.

I think you know how involved I've been with the School. I've served on the Board for nine years -- and have seen firsthand the great work they do. All of my children have gone there and have done wonders later on at college. They couldn't have had a better education than the one they received at Middleton. But you know that already, since your sons are in the School now.

We're in the early stages of launching a campaign to build a new Library and add to our Endowment. It's terribly exciting. I won't dwell on the particulars now but when we see you, we'll discuss it all in detail. I think you'll be as impressed with the program as I am.

We're not going to ask you for money. At least not on this visit! And I made Sandra promise that she wouldn't ask for a gift either.

All we want is an opportunity to talk about the program, ask for your good counsel and advice, and determine what might be appropriate next steps. If there aren't any next steps, that's up to you.

Thanks so much. I consider this a favor of the highest order and look forward to seeing you soon.

Sincerely,

Jean Smyth
Board Member
Middleton School

Jean Smyth
345 Carey Street
Middleton, OH 97348

Dear John and Jane:

You likely know how involved I've been with The Salvation Army in town. I've been a member of its board for five years but I've known about its work long before then.

In my judgment, it's one of the most effective organizations for reaching out to those with the greatest need. The Army has a loving arm it extends to the down-and-out, the misplaced, the homeless, and abused families. There's really no other organization quite like it in our community.

Captain John Guest is Commander of the Corps here. I have great admiration for his commitment and devotion.

We're about to launch a major campaign for a new Center for the Homeless. I've asked Capt. Guest to call on you.

I've made him promise that he won't be asking for a gift. You can count on that. But I do want him to tell you in detail about the Center and how important it is to our community and those who are served. I feel certain you're going to find the project as exciting as I do.

I've asked Capt. Guest to tell you about the project and get your good counsel and advice as to what steps might be taken next to move the program forward. And, by the way, if there are no further steps as far as you're concerned, that's entirely up to you!

Thanks so much. Capt. Guest's visit is so important and you're someone I particularly wanted him to meet. I'll consider this a favor of the highest order for you to see him. And that will be one I owe you!

Sincerely,

Jean Smyth
Board Member
Salvation Army

Jean Smyth
345 Carey Street
Middleton, OH 97348

Dear Peter and Mary:

You perhaps know that I've served on the Board of Trustees of Sacred Heart Hospital for a number of years. I consider it one of the most important institutions in our community.

I'll be calling in the next few days to set up a time when we might visit. I want to tell you about some exciting plans we have for the new Cancer Center. I feel certain you're going to find the concept as important as I do.

In my judgment, it's one of the most consequential programs we could possibly undertake in our community.

Have you had the same experience I've had -- friends and family who have died of the dreaded disease? Well, this new Center will be a critically important answer.

On this visit, I won't be asking for a gift. That's a promise! Later on, if the two of you decide to do something, that will be entirely up to you.

I do look forward to the visit. I'll be calling in the next few days.

Sincerely,

Jean Smyth
Board Member
Sacred Heart Hospital

Jean Smyth
345 Carey Street
Middleton, OH 97348

Dear Peter:

Thanks so much for arranging for our visit.

I'll be at your home next Wednesday evening at seven o'clock. Let's plan on no more than an hour together.

I'm really looking forward to being with you and Mary.

Sincerely,

Jean Smyth

More Objections and How to Respond

OBJECTION: *We already give to so many organizations. How can we make a large gift to the Hospital?*

RESPONSE: I know you give to a great deal in our community. The truth is, I probably wouldn't be calling on you if I didn't know how generous you are and how greatly you care.

My family and I considered the Hospital's campaign in light of a lot of other requests. We decided the Hospital simply has to be a priority at this time if we're going to get the kind of quality of service we've come to expect. I want that kind of care for my family and I want the kind of hospital this community deserves.

- *Or, Feel, Felt, Found*

I know how you *feel*. It seems to me there's no end to the number of times I'm called on to give to something or another. I *felt* the same way you do. But when I thought about how important this hospital is to my family and the community, I *found* I simply had to give this program priority. The Hospital is just that important to us.

OBJECTION: *Who said I should give this much?*

RESPONSE: I can assure you, no one's going to tell you how much to give. In fact, I'm not nearly smart enough to talk you into a gift you don't want to make. But it would have been impossible to plan this campaign and try to determine its success if we didn't have some idea how a number of our friends would respond.

So we got together a very small group who reviewed a number of our possible donors. We tried to determine what was a fair and appropriate amount to suggest. By the way, we've learned that a lot of folks don't really know what they should give and end up asking us what would be a proper donation.

This small group gave an assessment of each potential contributor. We added that all up and were able to determine that we're going to have a successful campaign.

But I can assure you, nobody is going to tell you what you should give. That decision is entirely yours and I respect that. No matter what amount you give, it will be important. But based on everything we've talked about and what you've done in the past....

• *Or, Feel, Felt, Found*

Boy, do I know how you *feel*. The first time I had someone tell me what they thought I ought to give,

I exploded. But then she explained to me that she wouldn't dare try to tell me what I should give. That was a decision entirely up to me. I guess I *felt* pretty much like you did -- no one is going to tell me what to do.

But then she went on to explain how important and urgent the program was and how important my gift would be to the success of the campaign and all the people served. I *found* that made a great deal of sense. And truthfully, I was wondering what I should do in terms of a gift. Her giving me an idea of what I might think about was actually pretty helpful.

OBJECTION: *The stock market has been crazy and my stuff has taken a real tumble.*

RESPONSE: I can certainly identify with that. I've had the same kind of issue in my own personal life. Keep in mind what we're asking for now is your intent of what you'd like to give. We have a form called a Letter of Intent. You can indicate what you would like to do for the future of the Hospital and this community.

As far as the timing is concerned, that'll be your decision and you can wait until you're feeling a little bit better about your stock.

What we need to know now is what you would like to do assuming the finances are there to back it up. Keep in mind that this Letter of Intent isn't a legally binding contract -- it's hardly that. It's simply an expression of your faith and belief in this program.

- *Or, Feel, Felt, Found*

I know how you *feel* about the stock. Everything in my portfolio seemed to go south. I *felt* exactly the way you do. And who knows how quickly things are going to turn around. If I had to make a gift during the next twelve months on a pledge, I simply wasn't going to do it.

But the folks in the campaign office talked with me and I *found* that I don't have to make a pledge. They just want me to indicate what I'd like to give. And I have control of the timing. If I don't feel I'm in a position to pay all or even part of what I've indicated, I'll let the Development Office know that. I have asked them to send me a reminder on a regular basis so that I don't lose track.

OBJECTION: *I never pledge.*

RESPONSE: Here's the best part of our program. We don't have legally binding pledges. What we're asking for is your intention of what you'd like to do over the next three years. Let's assume, for instance, that your health is good, the business is doing well, and the family is intact. What would you like to do for this important program?

We'll be able to record that and each year the Hospital will send you a reminder of what you've indicated. If for any reason you can't fulfill that part of your intention, simply let the Development Office know and that'll be the end of it.

And by the way, this intention of your gift doesn't encumber your estate in any way. We just need to know what you would like to do over the three years.

- *Or, Feel, Felt, Found*

I know how you *feel* about pledging. There's no way I'm able to see very far into the future either. I have no idea of what my income will be or what conditions will be like. I *felt* exactly the same way you do. Here's what I *found*. The Hospital suggested I simply indicate what I'd like to do, assuming the times ahead are good for me and my family. I care so much about the Hospital I was willing to extend myself in this way. I understand it's not legally binding but what I like about it is that they're still able to record my gift.

OBJECTION: *The cost of health care is so horribly high. I feel I get dinged even when I drive by the place!*

RESPONSE: The cost of health care is certainly high. But it's not easy providing proper care. It simply takes a great deal of money. And ours is one of the lowest cost hospitals in the whole state. On top of that, we take care of a lot of charity cases -- we've got to do that.

And of course, you know that insurance reimbursement only pays a portion of the cost. That's why this campaign is so important. We have no reserves we can use and we don't want to borrow the money and burden our future annual operations.

- *Or, Feel, Felt, Found*

I know how you *feel*. I was amazed at the cost

the last time I used the Emergency Room. I *felt* the charges were excessive but when I started doing some investigating and talked with some of the management, here's what I *found*.

They've cut their expenses at the Hospital to the very bone. I've looked into that and I'm convinced it's true. In fact, their costs are about as low as any hospital in the state -- and in my judgment, the service and quality are of the highest.

I also found that if we borrow money for this project, we're going to have to pay it back year after year, and that'll cause a terrible burden on everyone who uses the Hospital.

That's the trouble with borrowing money -- you have to pay it back. That's why this campaign is so important. It becomes an investment in the community and in our future.

OBJECTION: *I've been giving to the Hospital on an annual basis. Why don't you just take that gift and use it for the capital program. I don't really care where it goes.*

RESPONSE: Your gift to the annual campaign is essential. There are programs and services we simply couldn't provide if it weren't for the help you and others give us on an ongoing and annual basis.

This capital campaign is really for our future and the needs of this community into the next decade. I want you to continue giving annually. But let's talk again about this capital campaign.

• *Or, Feel, Felt, Found*

I know how you *feel* about that. We've been

giving to the hospital over the years and as a matter of fact, I thought it was a fairly good gift and that I was doing my share and maybe then some. I *felt* exactly the same way you do but let me tell you what I *found* when I began looking into the situation.

You probably didn't know this but the Hospital is pretty much on a pay-as-you-go basis. At the end of the year, the Hospital makes about two percent income over expenses. That's not the way it was before, but it's certainly the way things are now and it's getting worse.

That's why the Hospital depends greatly on your annual gifts. The more I looked into it, the more convinced I became that the annual gift was essential. I wouldn't touch that. But based on the need for this capital program, we decided to make a significant gift to the capital campaign.

•••

The objections I've posed here relate to a hospital. But they're almost exactly what you'll face for your university, the YMCA, the museum, or any cause. Review the responses. Use your own language. Make them your own. You'll be great.

Profile of a Major Gift Donor and How Much to Ask for

You'll find that the majority of your major gift donors fit a certain pattern. Oh certainly, there will be exceptions but look over this list. If your prospect meets most of the criteria -- you're well on your way to getting the gift. Here's the profile of a major gift donor:

1. Is of significant net worth. He or she is financially capable of making a large gift, the size you requested.

2. Has sufficient disposable income to make a large gift.

3. Believes strongly in the mission of your organization or is an advocate of the type of service you provide even though he or she might not be quite familiar with your organization.

4. Has been giving to you annually over a long period of time.

5. Has high philanthropic interest, intent, and experience.

6. Has or currently serves on the board and is an active volunteer.

7. Has few family commitments that will constrain the gift. For example, no alimony, has taken care of the grandchildren, no dependants or children living at home.

And here are three general "formulas" you might find helpful:

1. Ten percent of the prospect's annual income equals his giving ability over a five-year pledge period.

Example: 10 percent of $200,000 equals $20,000 which translates into a gift of $4,000 per year for five years.

2. Two to five percent of the prospect's net worth represents his giving over a five-year pledge period.

Example: $2 million net worth.
Two to five percent equals $40,000 to $100,000 which translates into a gift of $8,000 to $20,000 per year for five years.

3. Ten times annual income equals net worth.

Example: $200,000 (annual income) times 10 equals $2 million net worth.

CHARACTERTISTICS OF GIVING: ANNUAL GIVING VS MAJOR GIFTS

There's a distinct difference in the characteristics of an ongoing annual gift and the elements that exist in making a major gift. When you make your call, be aware of the components of each.

Annual Gift	Major Gift
For the ongoing work of the institution to sustain the service.	For endowment, special equipment, building programs.
Frequently asked for.	Infrequently asked for.
Regular annual gift.	10 to 25 times annual gift.
A quick decision.	More time needed.
Cerebral: "I'll go ahead and do this."	Visceral: a great joy in making the gift
Best done by a personal visit.	Personal visit always required.
Can be solicited alone	Best done in pairs, or more.
No need for professional help	May need attorney, accountant.
Spouse not always necessary for presentation	Spouse should be there for presentation.
Volunteer can handle	May be done with CEO or staff member, with volunteer
Can often be done on first visit	May require two or three visits and follow-up.
Out of income	Out of assets.
Cash gift	Extended over 3 to 5 years.
For the good of the institution	For the good it does in the life of the donor

Of Related Interest by Jerold Panas

Over the course of a storied career, Jerold Panas has worked with literally thousands of boards, from those governing the toniest of prep schools to those spearheading the local Y. He has counseled floundering groups; he has been the wind beneath the wings of boards whose organizations have soared.

In fact, it's a safe bet that Panas has observed more boards at work than perhaps anyone in America, all the while helping them to surpass campaign goals of $100,000 to $100 million.

Funnel every ounce of that experience and wisdom into a single book and what you have is *The Fundraising Habits of Supremely Successful Boards*, the brilliant culmination of what Panas has learned firsthand about boards who excel at the task of resource development.

Anyone who has read *Asking* or any of Panas' other books knows his style – a breezy and irresistible mix of storytelling, exhortation, and inspiration.

Fundraising Habits follows the same engaging mold, offering a panoply of habits any board would be wise to cultivate. Some are specific, with measurable outcomes. Others are more intangible, with Panas seeking to impart an attitude of success.

Here's just a sampling:
• You don't allow a mission deficit.
• You never lose sight that your organization is in the business of changing lives or saving lives.
• You're willing to leave the comfort zone.
• You understand that not all gifts are worth accepting.

In all, there are 25 habits and each is explored in two- and three-page chapters ... all of them animated by real-life stories only this grandmaster of philanthropy can tell.

From Emerson & Church, Publishers
www.emersonandchurch.com

Of Related Interest by Jerold Panas

How do you top perhaps the greatest selling fundraising book of all time? How do you improve upon *Mega Gifts*, a book CASE Currents magazine called "the most important fundraising book" written?

Quite simple really. You update the content, add more chapters, introduce a rash of new donors, and look anew at what's happened over the past two decades.

What you end up with is an even better book, if that's possible, with brand new material.

The Second Edition of *Mega Gifts: Who Gives Them, Who Gets Them* is no 'how-to' book. Panas would wince at such a characterization. No, *Mega Gifts* is far more substantive and significant than that. What Panas is after is nothing less than exposing the heart and soul of those who make large gifts.

And in his own inimitable style, he goes right to the source, the big givers themselves, and speaks at length with dozens of them. Then, to corroborate what he learns, Panas surveys nearly a thousand professionals in the field and incorporates their insights as well.

What you find in *Mega Gifts* is the real deal, from the primary source. This isn't conjecture. And what you gain is:

• An understanding of donors' innermost motivations
• What drives them to the causes they support
• How they reach their decision
• What nurtures their loyalty
• What they expect from organizations and their staff
• How they wish to be recognized
• Even how they want you to approach them

The result is a tour de force book from an unrivalled storyteller, with insights dancing off every page. In fact, there's so much inside information, you'll feel you're reading someone else's mail.

Mega Gifts is the 800 pound gorilla in the field ... and one hugely entertaining animal it is.

From Emerson & Church, Publishers
www.emersonandchurch.com

ABOUT THE AUTHOR

In *Born to Raise*, the author wrote: "Someone once told me that my career would have five stages: 1) Who is Jerry Panas? 2) Get me Jerry Panas, 3) We need someone like Jerry Panas, 4) What we need is a young Jerry Panas, and 5) Who is Jerry Panas?"

Jerry believes he's somewhere between stages two and three. "But," he says, "my friends indicate I'm somewhere in stage four, quickly approaching stage five!"

Hailed in Newsweek as "the Robert Schuller of fundraising," Jerry is the author of seven books, many of them classics in the field. He's also a popular columnist for *Contributions* magazine and a familiar and favorite speaker at conferences and workshops throughout the nation.

A senior officer of one of America's premier fundraising firms, Jerry lives with his wife, Felicity, in northwest Connecticut.

Copies of this book are available from
the publisher at discount when purchased
in quantity for boards of directors,
volunteers, or staff.

Emerson
& Church
PUBLISHERS

P.O. Box 338 • Medfield, MA 02052
Tel. 508-359-0019 • Fax 508-359-2703